LAU C

Richard Avent MA, FSA

Contents

Series Editor David M. Robinson *BSc, PhD, FSA*
Designed by Joanna Griffiths

First Published 1995

Printed in Great Britain by Empress Litho

ISBN 1 85760 066 5

INTRODUCTION

The modern traveller through south Wales speeds past town and over river, barely aware of forest, hill, or valley. For our medieval predecessors, it would have been a very different story. Contemplating a journey from east to west, there were two options. The longer route lay to the north of the mountains and their deep-cut valleys, westwards along the upper reaches of the River Usk, and then down the Vale of Tywi to Carmarthen. Or, the traveller could take the shorter, but tortuous coastal route, fording or being ferried across one river mouth after another.

Close to the points where these rivers met the sea, the Normans had established a string of fortifications, stretching from Chepstow in the east to Pembroke in the west. Each castle controlled its river crossing and guarded a waterborne routeway leading into the heart of south Wales. The garrison could, if needed, be supplied by sea. The castle served as the administrative centre of a lordship, sometimes with a town, a priory, and port, or at least some form of simple harbourage.

Laugharne, at the mouth of the River Taf, south-west of Carmarthen, was one of these coastal strongholds. Like its neighbours to the east, at Llansteffan and Kidwelly, it was first established as an earthwork castle in the early twelfth century. Following the pattern seen at other Anglo-Norman castles in Wales, the de Brian family was to develop Laugharne into a fully-fledged stone construction by the late thirteenth century. Towards the end of the sixteenth century, the castle was rescued from near ruin by the Elizabethan courtier, Sir John Perrot (d. 1592), who converted it into a fine Tudor mansion. This renaissance in its fortunes was short-lived. Late in 1644, during the Civil War, it succumbed to Parliamentarian gunfire and siege, was captured and partially dismantled, never to be occupied again.

The long and often turbulent history of Laugharne Castle is traced in this guide. The text draws on the evidence of extensive archaeological excavations carried out from 1976 to 1993. Our current understanding of Laugharne is also based on a detailed study of the upstanding structure together with a close assessment of the documentary sources. This analysis continues, and it may be possible to refine our conclusions yet further for future editions of this guidebook.

Laugharne Castle, at the mouth of the River Taf, was first established in the early twelfth century. The stone castle was developed by the de Brian family in the thirteenth and fourteenth centuries, and in the sixteenth century it was rescued from near ruin by the Elizabethan courtier, Sir John Perrot.

A HISTORY OF THE CASTLE

BEFORE THE CASTLE

During the archaeological excavations at the castle, it was possible to trace the very earliest human activity on the site in several small areas. It became clear that this activity began long before the arrival of the first Norman castle, and that it occurred in a sequence of phases. Accurate dating of these phases, however, proved difficult.The initial periods of occupation were represented by traces of postholes and gullies, perhaps associated with timber buildings. Above these, within a ploughsoil, there were sherds of abraded Roman pottery. In places, grooves – which had been cut into the ground by the ploughshare – could still be detected. There followed a phase when there appears to have been little activity on the site. Finally, a low bank was constructed at the eastern end of the later inner ward.

The Roman pottery was the only material which could provide an indication of date. And it is possible that some of the early occupation at Laugharne may belong to the Romano-British era. Alternatively, as the pottery sherds were worn and abraded, they may have found their way into the ploughsoil as part of the manuring of fields. In this context, it is interesting to note that just above the cliff, on the hillside at Glan-y-môr, to the north-east of the castle, there is a semi-circular earthwork enclosure. Pottery found at this site suggests that it may have been a settlement dating to the late prehistoric and possibly Roman periods. The headland, upon which the castle now stands, could therefore have been periodically ploughed as land associated with the Glan-y-môr earthwork. As for the bank beneath the later inner ward, again dating is a problem, though it may have formed part of some non-military boundary.

THE TWELFTH AND EARLY THIRTEENTH CENTURIES

In the 1090s the Normans overran a politically divided west Wales, establishing castles at Cardigan, Pembroke, and Rhydygors (near Carmarthen). These initial successes met with a major setback later that decade when the Welsh drove the conquerors from all their newly

The Normans overran a politically divided west Wales in the 1090s, establishing castles as footholds in the newly-conquered lands. By 1135, most of lowland southern Wales was firmly under Norman control. This scene from the Bayeux Tapestry shows an earthwork castle under construction.

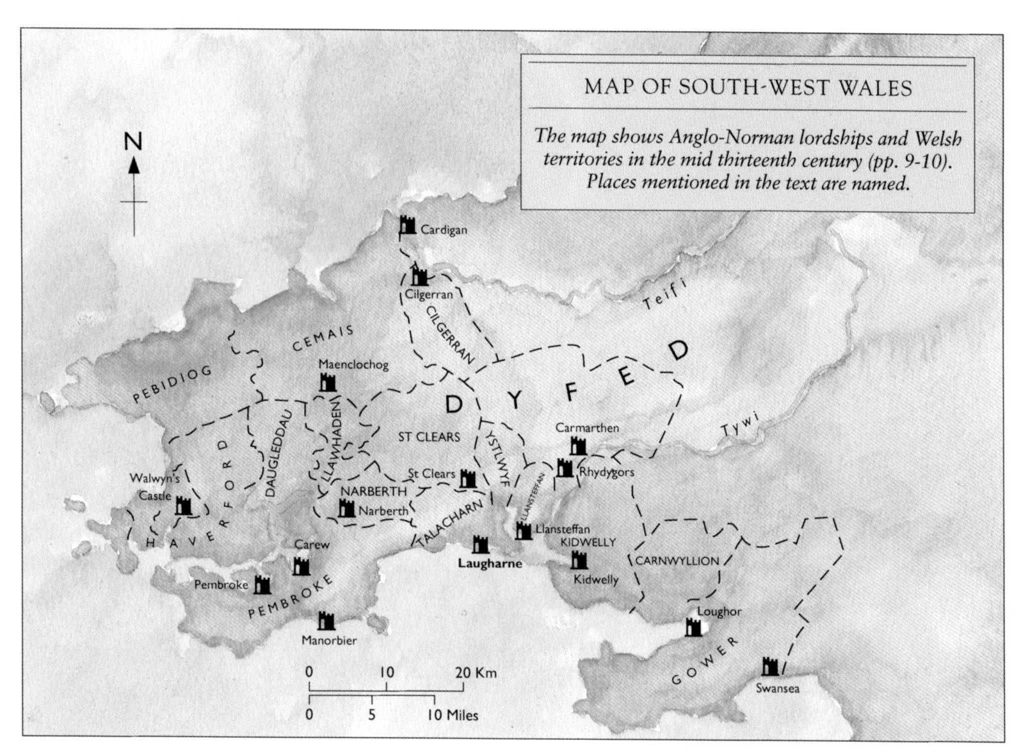

MAP OF SOUTH-WEST WALES

The map shows Anglo-Norman lordships and Welsh territories in the mid thirteenth century (pp. 9-10). Places mentioned in the text are named.

established strongholds, with the exception of Pembroke. The pendulum of fortune was to swing back, and in the early years of the twelfth century Norman control was re-established in the regions of Ystrad Tywi and eastern Dyfed (see map). Carmarthen was to become the centre of the royal honour and a base for consolidating the power of the English king. Over the next few years, Carmarthen developed as the centre of a new administrative unit which was to include Laugharne near its westernmost boundary.

By the time of King Henry I's death in 1135, most of the lowland in southern Wales was firmly under Norman control with a network of castles and the establishment of the first boroughs. The new castle of Bishop Roger of Salisbury (d. 1139) at Kidwelly, for example, is mentioned in 1114, whilst the earliest reference to a castle at Laugharne probably comes from 1116. In that year, *Brut y Tywysogyon* (*Chronicle of the Princes*) records that Bleddyn ap Cedifor was entrusted with 'the castle of Robert Courtemain, which was at Abercorram'. Bleddyn appears to be an early example of a Welshman who not only sided with the Normans but was sufficiently well regarded to take charge of one of their castles. Laugharne stands at a point where a small stream, the Coran, enters the River Taf. *Aber* is the Welsh word for the mouth of a river and *corram* may be an earlier form of Coran. Throughout the twelfth and thirteenth centuries the names of *Abercorram* and *Talacharn* (the Welsh for Laugharne) both appear in *Brut y Tywysogyon*, and it seems likely – though not certain – that they refer to the same site at Laugharne.

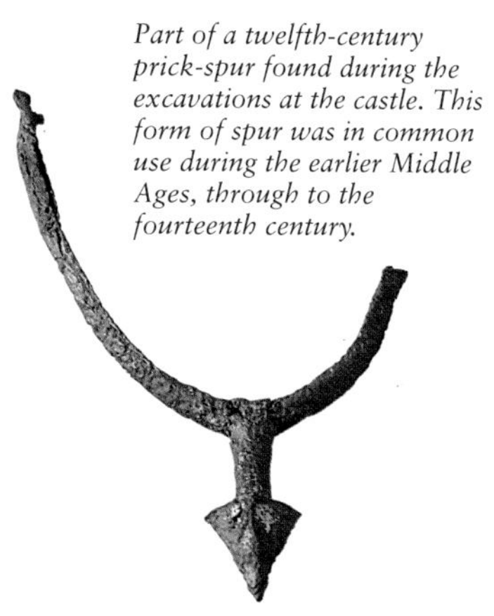

Part of a twelfth-century prick-spur found during the excavations at the castle. This form of spur was in common use during the earlier Middle Ages, through to the fourteenth century.

The Welsh Chronicle of the Princes *(*Brut y Tywysogyon*) records a castle at Abercorram - which is probably Laugharne - in 1116 (By courtesy of the National Library of Wales, Peniarth Ms. 20, p. 130).*

The earliest Norman castle at Laugharne was probably of the form known as a 'ringwork', as at neighbouring Llansteffan and Kidwelly. At Llansteffan (above) the ringwork is marked by the later inner ward, to the right of this view. At Kidwelly (right), the sweeping line of the outer curtain wall marks the position of the ringwork bank. All three castles were to become fully developed stone strongholds.

The archaeological evidence for the earliest medieval stronghold at Laugharne comes from those same limited areas which produced traces of pre-castle activity. As at neighbouring Kidwelly and Llansteffan, the early Norman castle appears to have been of a form known as a 'ringwork'. It was a relatively simple enclosure, in this case with the coastline and river mouth forming natural strength to the south and west, but with man-made defences on the northern landward side of the ridge. It was on this more vulnerable inland side that the builders threw up an earthen bank. This would have been surmounted by either a timber palisade, or a stone wall, and was fronted by an external ditch.

The western end of this ditch was discovered during the archaeological work. It lay beneath the now lawned garden in the outer ward (p. 27), with its base as much as 23 feet (7m) lower than the present ground surface. The precise line of the ditch is unknown but it may have extended, up what was then a long slope, to a point outside the surviving later outer gatehouse. Sweeping east, its alignment may not have been very different from the later stone curtain wall. In the north-eastern corner of the castle, the slight remains of a clay bank, found just behind the later ditch, may be all that remains of the Norman ringwork bank.

As reconstructed, the plan would have been unusually large for a ringwork enclosure. In part, this may be accounted for by the need to accommodate what was then a steep slope on the western side of the ridge extending down to the Coran. An additional line of defence might have existed at the top of this slope, roughly on a line between the two later gatehouses. Alternatively, the excavated section of ditch may be that for an outer bailey, with an inner bailey occupying the area of the later inner ward, though as yet there is no hard evidence to confirm this theory.

We can say very little of the internal ringwork buildings at Laugharne. In one small area of the later inner ward, a circular clay hearth was found. About six and a half feet (2m) across, it lay within a building which was probably of high status. The building could have been a hall, though the walls lay outside the excavated area. The hearth was renewed on two occasions suggesting a fairly lengthy period of use. It was scientifically dated (using a technique known as archaeomagnetic dating) to the twelfth century.

In the twenty or so years following the death of Henry I, Norman ambitions in south-west Wales were to witness a major setback. This was a period which saw the revival of the Welsh kingdom of

Deheubarth and, eventually, the rise of Rhys ap Gruffudd (d. 1197). The Lord Rhys, as he is generally known, was to dominate the political scene in west Wales throughout the second half of the twelfth century. After almost two decades of uncertainty and periodic hostility, Rhys and King Henry II (1154-89) reached an accord, sealed in negotiations at Pembroke and Laugharne in 1171-72. Their meeting at Laugharne presumably took place at the castle. Under the accord, Rhys was to acknowledge his client status to the English Crown. In return, the king appointed Rhys 'justice on his behalf in all Deheubarth'. Henceforward, 'Rhys the Great', 'Rhys the Good', was to tower in the political history of the region, and fully deserved the title he claimed for himself as 'rightful prince of south Wales'.

On the king's death in 1189, the fragility in the personal nature of the accord between the two men was fully exposed, with the government of the new king choosing to ignore the delicacy of the situation.

This fourteenth-century effigy in St Davids Cathedral is generally taken to represent Rhys ap Gruffudd (d. 1197). The Lord Rhys, as he is known, met King Henry II at Laugharne and Pembroke in 1171-72, when the two men reached an accord. At Laugharne, they probably met at the castle.

King Henry II (1154-89) was to appoint the Lord Rhys 'justice on his behalf in all Deheubarth'. The red-haired king is seen in this illumination from a twelfth-century manuscript (By courtesy of the National Library of Ireland, Ms. 700).

Rhys's response was swift and merciless: he waged war, attacking and capturing the Anglo-Norman castles at Laugharne, Llansteffan and St Clears.

These episodes are of particular interest in that there is some evidence to suggest that the first phase in Laugharne's history ended with a fire. The fire may well have been associated with Rhys's attack of 1189. Certainly, at some point during the second half of the twelfth century, the castle was extensively remodelled. It was then, if not before, that the northern defences were quite definitely to become those of an outer bailey. A bank, probably with an outer ditch, was constructed on approximately the same line as the later inner ward enclosure. A large rectangular stone building, some 33 feet (10m) wide and in excess of 53 feet (16m) long, filled the northern half of the inner bailey. The new building was probably a two-storey construction, with a hall on the first floor, and may have been similar in

THE PHASE 2 CASTLE

LATE TWELFTH – EARLY THIRTEENTH CENTURY

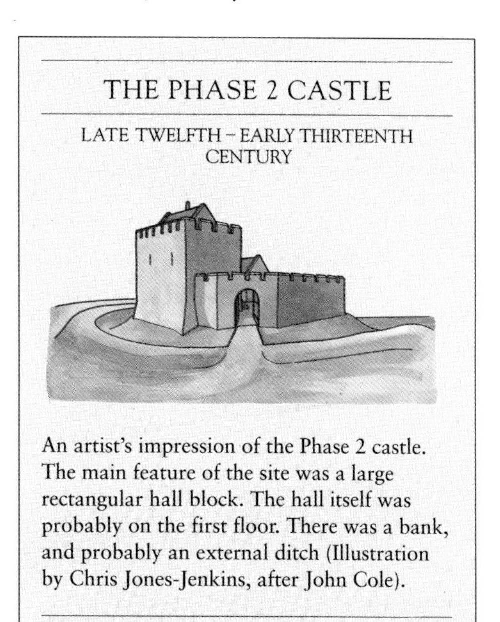

An artist's impression of the Phase 2 castle. The main feature of the site was a large rectangular hall block. The hall itself was probably on the first floor. There was a bank, and probably an external ditch (Illustration by Chris Jones-Jenkins, after John Cole).

A twelfth-century Norman hall block survives at Manorbier Castle, Pembrokeshire. The excavated building at Laugharne must have appeared very similar in scale and proportions.

appearance to the surviving twelfth-century hall block at Manorbier Castle further to the west in Pembrokeshire. Some evidence was found of other buildings of this period in the south-eastern part of the inner bailey.

Laugharne Castle was subsequently recovered after its capture in 1189. But, by the end of the twelfth century, the Anglo-Norman lords seemed to have realized that, so long as the Welsh were able to produce great leaders like the Lord Rhys, the total conquest of Wales was, for the time being, beyond their reach. In south-west Wales, Anglo-Norman control had become firmly established in the lordships of Haverford, Wiston, Pembroke and southern Gower, but it remained precarious further away from this heartland in the lordships of Cemais, Cilgerran, St Clears, Laugharne, Llansteffan, Kidwelly, Carnwyllion and northern Gower.

The precariousness of the situation was further demonstrated in 1215. Shortly before Christmas, the Anglo-Norman lords of the March were left reeling after a bloody and devastating three-week campaign by the Welsh. It was a campaign of truly national character, with the Welsh uniting under the brilliant prince of Gwynedd, Llywelyn ab Iorwerth (d. 1240). They swept the marcher lords from their main castles at Carmarthen and Cardigan, taking a string of other southern strongholds. As the chronicler of *Brut y Tywysogyon* tells us, Llywelyn's forces 'overthrew to the ground Llansteffan, St Clears and Laugharne'.

Once again these events are of direct significance for the building history of the castle since, during the second phase in the history of Laugharne, we know the castle suffered from a catastrophic event. Buildings were burnt to the ground, and the discovery of numerous arrowheads and a spearhead, along with damaged artefacts, all seem to point to an attack on the castle. This may have been the 1215 attack by the forces of Llywelyn ab Iorwerth. In 1223 William Marshal the younger (d. 1231) recovered Cardigan and Carmarthen castles from the Welsh, and Laugharne may also have been restored to its owner as part of that campaign.

Our archaeological evidence for the castle in the period immediately after 1215 is very limited within the inner ward. Much of the ground surface was levelled down during the later Tudor era, destroying any traces which may have survived. However, a small circular or semi-circular stone bastion or tower was constructed at the western end of the outer bailey ditch, either at this time or towards the end of the previous phase. This in turn was subsequently demolished and replaced by a rectangular building with an oven.

A spearhead found during the excavations at Laugharne. Its discovery associated with buildings burnt to the ground suggests it may have used at the time of the attack on the castle in 1215.

THE CASTLE UNDER THE DE BRIANS

In 1247, Guy de Brian received a grant from the king to hold a yearly fair at 'his manor of Talachar'. This is the earliest reference to the family which was to own the castle until the late fourteenth century. It was the de Brians who were responsible for building the stone castle which was later to be converted into a Tudor mansion.

The first in a long succession of Guy de Brians appears in the middle of the twelfth century in south Devon. Torbryan, between the rivers Teign and Dart, became the family home. By the death of the seventh, and last, Guy de Brian in 1390, the family landholdings had extended not only into south-west Wales but east into Somerset and as far north as the Forest of Dean and Tewkesbury.

It appears to have been the fourth Guy de Brian who established the family in south-west Wales. He acquired the lordships of Laugharne, and that of Walwyn's Castle in the west of Pembrokeshire. Although we know that Guy de Brian IV held Laugharne by 1247, we cannot provide a more precise date for the family's acquisition of these lordships. What is certain is that he must have been faced with a castle that was not only in need of repair but was also outdated by the military standards of the day.

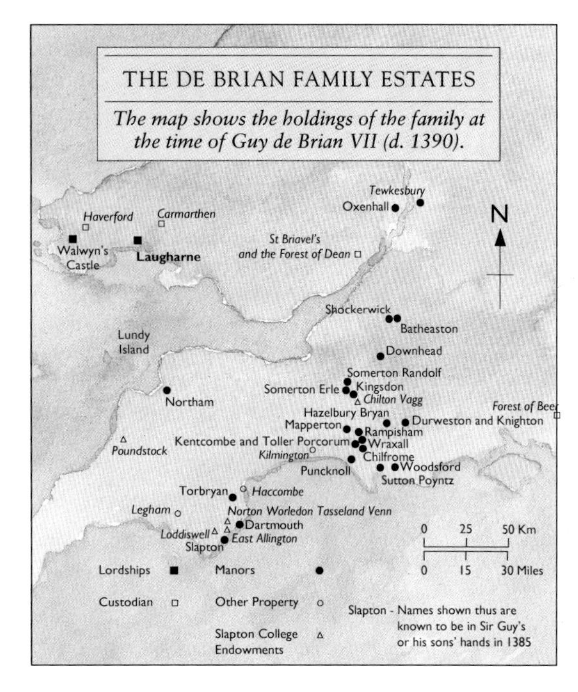

Right: *The de Brian family arms from the tomb chest of Guy de Brian VII in Tewkesbury Abbey (By kind permission of the vicar and churchwardens, Tewkesbury Abbey).*

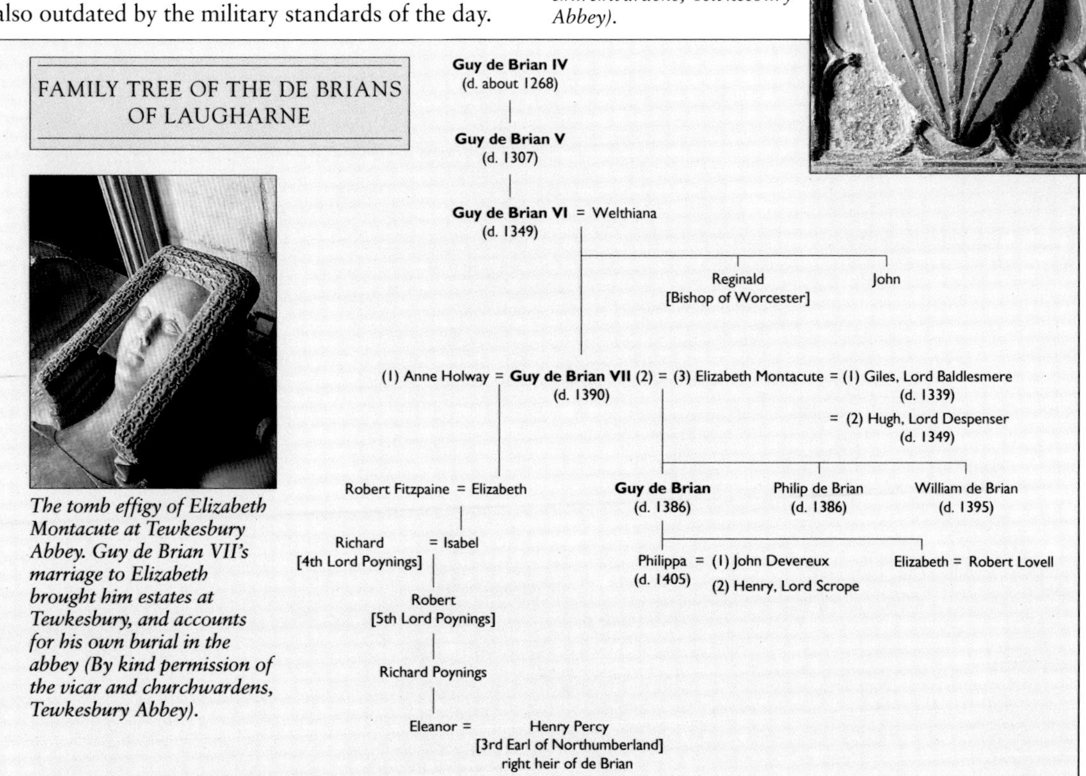

The tomb effigy of Elizabeth Montacute at Tewkesbury Abbey. Guy de Brian VII's marriage to Elizabeth brought him estates at Tewkesbury, and accounts for his own burial in the abbey (By kind permission of the vicar and churchwardens, Tewkesbury Abbey).

His reconstruction marks the third phase in the castle's history and the first stage in the development of the upstanding structure as we see it today.

Before his death about 1268, de Brian created a new inner ward for the castle, removing all earlier structures. The principal landward defence consisted of two round towers linked to one another by a curtain wall. The wall extended southwards to the low cliff above the river, and then along its edge. The western stretch of curtain was pierced by a plain entrance overlooked by, and guarded from, the north-west tower. An external ditch, extending from cliff edge to cliff edge, completed the defensive arrangements. The larger, austere, north-west tower, with its unlit basement, three upper storeys, and stone-vaulted dome, served as the principal tower or keep of the castle. A hall was constructed against the southern, seaward-facing, curtain wall.

It seems likely that during this first phase in the castle's reconstruction, de Brian concentrated his efforts on the inner ward. He may have relied upon the pre-existing, or upgraded, timber defences of the outer ward to provide a defensive enclosure within which the new building works could take place.

An interesting comparison can be drawn between the design of the mid thirteenth-century inner ward at Laugharne and the somewhat earlier castle at Cilgerran in Pembrokeshire. Both castles were built on natural promontories, and in both cases the landward approach to the inner ward was defended by two substantial round towers.

There is an interesting comparison to be made between Laugharne in the mid thirteenth century and the somewhat earlier castle here at Cilgerran. Both had two substantial round towers defending their landward approach.

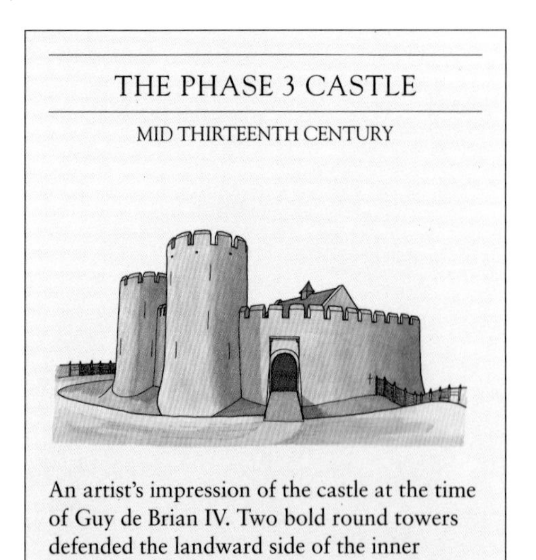

An artist's impression of the castle at the time of Guy de Brian IV. Two bold round towers defended the landward side of the inner ward. A plain gate through the curtain wall formed the principal entrance (Illustration by Chris Jones-Jenkins, after John Cole).

From 1255 onwards, native Wales was once again united under the leadership of a Gwynedd prince, the masterful Llywelyn ap Gruffudd (d. 1282). During 1257 and 1258, after years of simmering resentment, the Welsh erupted into all out attack. In one episode after another, they overran the English controlled territories of the southern and eastern March. In June 1257 an English force under Stephen Bauzan suffered a devastating defeat in the Tywi Valley. The Welsh went on to attack and burn the castle and town of *Abercorram* along with other castles and towns in west Wales, at Llansteffan, Narberth and Maenclochog.

Guy de Brian was taken by the Welsh, perhaps at the capture of Laugharne itself, or in any case soon afterwards. His release, probably during the first half of 1258, was only secured upon the payment of a ransom raised by his tenants with a contribution from the king. He was to die some ten years later, around 1268.

During the tenure of his son, Guy de Brian V, Laugharne was to enter the fourth phase in its history. The defences of both the inner and outer wards were to be strengthened and the overall level of accommodation improved. A gatehouse, with a single upper storey, was added to the earlier plain entrance into the inner ward. The south-west corner was strengthened by the provision of a round tower, and a new curtain wall was built along the southern side of the inner ward. It was also during this period that the defences of the outer ward were reconstructed in stone, along much the same line as today's outer boundary of the castle.

Within the overall scheme of Guy V, the design of the new outer gatehouse, with its well-carved stone dressings, stands out as a rather more advanced element. Its sophistication when compared to the inner ward gate, for example, could reflect a slight difference in date. Alternatively, there may have been a deliberate intention to focus more effort on the gatehouse facing de Brian's borough outside the castle walls. Indeed, it was probably Guy V who granted the town its borough charter. Laugharne Corporation still operates under this charter today.

THE PHASE 4 CASTLE

LATE THIRTEENTH CENTURY

An artist's impression of the castle at the time of Guy de Brian V. The defences were strengthened, the accommodation improved, and a projecting gatehouse was added to the inner ward (Illustration by Chris Jones-Jenkins, after John Cole).

It was probably Guy de Brian V (d. 1307) who granted the borough of Laugharne its present charter. Laugharne Corporation still operates under the charter today (By courtesy of Laugharne Corporation and Carmarthenshire Record Office, Laugharne 204).

The sixth of the Guy de Brians (d. 1349) succeeded his father to the lordship in 1307. He does not seem to have been a great builder, and we cannot link any of the castle features to his tenure with certainty. In about 1330, as a result of frailty, perhaps verging on insanity, the management of his south Wales estates was handed over to his son. Nineteen years later, Guy VII (d. 1390) formally inherited the lordship of Laugharne. The last in a long line of de Brians, he was also the most powerful and influential member of his family. Guy VII was to become a distinguished soldier and civil servant and a close confidant of King Edward III (1327-77). He rose to the position of Admiral of the Fleet, was employed as an ambassador on six occasions and was made a Knight of the Garter in 1370.

Right: *The seal of Guy de Brian VII, 1383 (Copyright: Public Record Office, DL 27/141).*

The degree and nature of the work undertaken at Laugharne by Guy de Brian VII suggests that part of the castle must have been in a poor state of repair by the middle of the fourteenth century. He set about modernizing and greatly improving the overall standard of accommodation. Much of the outer gatehouse was refaced, the inner gatehouse and south-western tower were heightened and the upper part of the entire western end of the inner ward rebuilt. A new south-east tower and postern entrance were constructed at the eastern end of the southern curtain. The opportunity was taken to enlarge the hall by extending it further to the east.

Contemporary documentary references to the castle are somewhat rare, though we do know that shortly before Guy VII's death his youngest son, William, was in residence. It was in 1389 that William acted as host, greeting the receiver general of the Mortimer family estates, Walter Brugge, at Laugharne. Brugge would have been entertained in a building that was handsomely appointed, combining strong defences with what would have been regarded, by the standards of the day, as a high level of accommodation.

Left: *Guy VII was the last in a long line of de Brians. He was the most powerful and influential member of his family, becoming a distinguished soldier and a Knight of the Garter. He was effectively to hold Laugharne from about 1330 until his death in 1390. Guy VII was buried at Tewkesbury Abbey where his tomb effigy now lies (By kind permission of the vicar and churchwardens, Tewkesbury Abbey).*

Sir Guy de Brian VII, Knight Garter 1370-90, distinguished himself in wars with Scotland, Flanders and France. He fought at the battle of Crécy, 1346, depicted here in a manuscript illumination from the Mémories de Philippe de Commines *(By courtesy of the Musée Dobree, Nantes, Ms. 18 fol. 73v. Photograph by Giraudon)*

THE PHASE 5 CASTLE

LATE FOURTEENTH CENTURY

An artist's impression of the castle as modified by Guy de Brian VII. The inner gatehouse and south-western tower were heightened, and the overall standard of accommodation improved (Illustration by Chris Jones-Jenkins, after John Cole).

Guy de Brian VII died in the following year. He had outlived his two eldest sons, though William, the youngest of the brood and the black sheep of the family, was to survive his father by five years. It was, however, the daughters of the older brothers who were to take precedence as successors to the de Brian estates. The next century was taken up with inheritance disputes and this, combined with the declining need for castles as residences, suggests that little more than the most basic maintenance would have taken place at the castle.

Below: *An artist's impression of the castle and town of Laugharne in the middle of the fourteenth century (Illustration by Ivan Lapper, 1994).*

Right: *The same view of the castle and town as it appears today .*

THE FIFTEENTH CENTURY

In 1403, King Henry IV (1399-1413) issued a writ instructing one Henry Lescrope to ensure that the defences at Laugharne were put in good order against the threat of attack from the troops of Owain Glyndŵr. This suggests that the castle must have been in a reasonably defensible state at that time. From 1448 the constables of the castle received a fee of twenty shillings a year. In 1464 a licence was granted for the castle and town to be walled, crenellated, and ditched. The townsfolk do not seem to have taken advantage of the licence since the borough defences always appear to have been of earth and timber.

Eventually, in 1488, agreement was reached between the four claimants to the de Brian inheritance, with Laugharne passing into the hands of Henry Percy, fourth earl of Northumberland (d. 1489). No major work appears to have taken place at the castle during the Northumberland period of ownership. Some minor repairs were carried out on a number of buildings including the outer gatehouse and the north-west tower. There emerges a general picture of a fairly ruinous stronghold, parts of which were maintained to provide limited accommodation for a sub-constable who, in the 1520s, was paid forty shillings a year for the custody of the castle and gaol.

An early sixteenth-century seal of the earls of Northumberland. Laugharne passed to the Northumberlands in 1488, and the family held it through to the mid sixteenth century (Copyright: Public Record Office, E 329/367).

THE SIXTEENTH CENTURY

In June 1531, the sixth earl of Northumberland (d. 1537), a weak and gullible man, entered into an agreement with Thomas Perrot, a leading member of the Pembrokeshire gentry. Perrot and his heirs were to receive the lordships of Laugharne and Walwyn's Castle for an annual rent of £80. In return, Perrot relinquished his seemingly groundless claims to the de Brian estates in Dorset, Somerset, and Devon. In September of that year, before the agreement could be confirmed, Thomas died aged only twenty-six. His heir, John, was just three years old.

In 1535 the earl of Northumberland sold the lordships of Laugharne and Walwyn's Castle to the king. Twelve years later, in the reign of Queen Mary (1553-58), they were granted back to Thomas, seventh earl of Northumberland (d. 1572). The castle is next heard of in 1560 when Queen Elizabeth I (1558-1603) granted it to James Reed, a local landowner. And from Reed, in 1575, the queen granted it on to Sir John Perrot at an annual rent of £80, still to be paid to the earls of Northumberland. Reed appears to have been in financial difficulties during the 1560s and early 1570s and sold some of his land to Perrot at that time. He was later employed by Perrot, apparently to act as his land agent. Finally, in 1584, Queen Elizabeth confirmed Perrot's tenancy of Laugharne by deed of settlement.

A portrait of Sir John Perrot (1528-92). Sir John was granted Laugharne by Queen Elizabeth I in 1575. He rescued the castle from near ruin and converted it into a fine Tudor residence (By kind permission of his lordship, the sixth Baron Hampton. Photograph supplied by Dr Roger Turvey).

THE TUDOR MANSION

It is clear from a survey of 1592 (p. 39), conducted at the time of Perrot's conviction for treason, that the castle was in a ruinous state when it first came into his ownership almost eighteen years earlier. It is also clear from the archaeological evidence that Perrot's conversion of the castle into a fine Tudor mansion took place in two stages. This is rather puzzling given the short time of his ownership. One explanation may be that the initial phase of work dates to the period after Perrot was first granted the castle in 1575. The building programme may then have been extended after his tenancy was confirmed in 1584. The 1592 survey indicates that Perrot did not quite complete his scheme at the castle, and that the quality of the workmanship was sub-standard.

SIR JOHN PERROT

John Perrot was born in November 1528, introduced to Court in the autumn of 1549 and knighted within a week of achieving his majority in November of that year. He was a staunch Protestant during the reign of Queen Mary (1553-58), eventually deciding that it was wiser to leave the country and join a military expedition in France. Despite this, and after five years of lobbying, Mary granted Perrot the castle and lordship of Carew.

With Mary's death, Perrot's fortunes changed. He was favoured by Queen Elizabeth I (1558-1603) and divided his time during the 1560s between the Court and Pembrokeshire, where he consolidated his power base. A man of somewhat fiery temperament, he had no difficulty in acquiring enemies both at Court and in south-west Wales.

In 1571, the queen appointed Perrot as the first lord of Munster. He returned in 1573, worn out from his experience but after what appear to have been two relatively successful years in Ireland. He then largely withdrew from public life spending much of the next ten years developing his estates in Pembrokeshire. In 1584 the queen appointed Perrot Lord Deputy of Ireland.

Perrot's time in Ireland as Lord Deputy, like that of those who had gone before and were to succeed him, was not an easy one. It is a measure of his ability that he was able to return in 1588 with his reputation, if not his health, intact. However, his absence had provided an opportunity for his enemies, both in Court and elsewhere, to conspire against him. In March 1591 he was imprisoned in the Tower. Found guilty on a charge of high treason, he was condemned to death on 27 April 1592. He died of ill health (although there is a suggestion that he may have been poisoned) on 3 November that year before sentence could be carried out. There is some evidence that the queen may have been on the point of pardoning him.

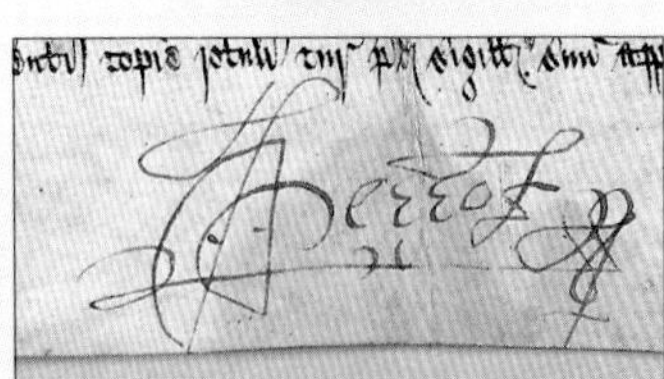

Top: *A carved stone head believed to represent Sir John Perrot, and thought to have come from Laugharne Castle (By courtesy of Carmarthen Museum).*

Above: *Sir John Perrot's signature, 1581 (By courtesy of Carmarthenshire Record Office, Cawdor/Lort, 17/683).*

Sir John Perrot was granted the lordship and castle of Carew by Queen Mary. This range of buildings along the north side of the castle was raised in grand Elizabethan style by Perrot.

Sir John Perrot was transforming the castles at Carew and Laugharne at a time when there was a great revival of chivalry. Tournaments and tilts were a popular form of entertainment (By courtesy of the College of Arms, Great Tournament Roll).

Sir John Perrot's conversion of a medieval castle into a mansion of some pretension needs to be seen in two contexts. First, the castle continued to symbolize 'lordship'. Although the concept of a gentlemen's home being his castle was by this time outmoded, if he was fortunate enough to have a strongly defended building, then there was much to be said for at least not substantially weakening it. This attitude seems to have governed the schemes adopted by Perrot at both Laugharne and Carew castles. Secondly, this was also the great age in the revival of chivalry, with Accession Day tilts at their height in the 1580s and 1590s. Indeed, it was in 1590 that Spenser's *The Faerie Queene* was published with its theme of devotion to a virgin ruler. Not only were stone castles Gothicized but, for particular tournaments and occasions of pageantry, mock wooden and even cardboard castles were built.

Sir John Perrot was much favoured by Queen Elizabeth I (1558-1603). In 1584, the queen was to appoint him Lord Deputy of Ireland. He returned in 1588, ill, but with his reputation intact. This portrait of the queen is by or after G. Gower, about 1588 (By courtesy of the National Portrait Gallery).

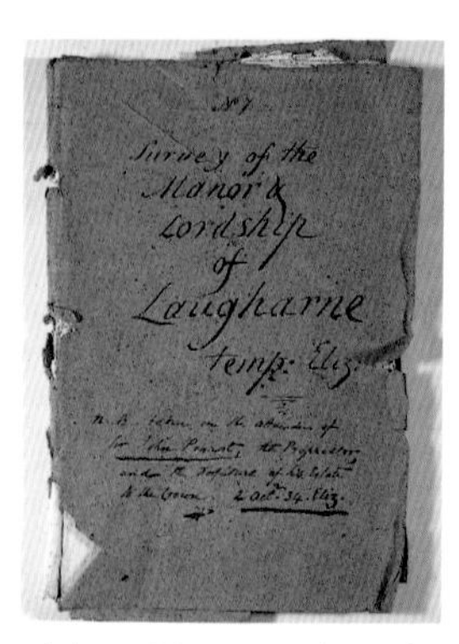

Survey of the
Manor &
Lordship
of
Laugharne
temp: Eliz.

The cover of the 1592 survey of Laugharne which was conducted at the time of Sir John Perrot's conviction for treason (By courtesy of Laugharne Corporation and Carmarthenshire Record Office, Laugharne 211).

A finely-carved stone capital now in Carmarthen Museum. It is believed to have come from Laugharne Castle and dates from the Tudor period (By courtesy of Carmarthen Museum).

No sooner had Perrot been convicted than parts of Laugharne Castle, particularly the wooden panelling, were being illegally removed and had to be returned by order of the Crown. Following Perrot's death in November 1592, his son, Sir Thomas, was restored to some of the family estates. He enjoyed these for just a short period, dying two years after his father.

THE PHASE 6 CASTLE

LATER SIXTEENTH CENTURY

An artist's impression of the castle as converted to a Tudor residence by Sir John Perrot. The medieval stronghold was to become a mansion of some pretension (Illustration by Chris Jones-Jenkins, after John Cole).

EARLY SEVENTEENTH CENTURY

From 1592 until 1627, when it became the property of Sir Sackville Crowe, the lordship of Laugharne had a turbulent history. Still leased from the Northumberland family, it frequently changed hands and was the source of constant legal disputes.

In April 1615 a Special Commission was sent from the Court of the Exchequer to survey the castle. The commissioners were unable to gain access, but they could see that:

'... *the ffreestone windowes, the iron barres, the glasse and leades are taken downe, for we might perceave, the rooffe of the chappell being spatious, and formerly covered with leade to be bare, the leade by the procuremente, of the said Rees Ritherch esquier ripped upe taken away.*

... *It hath beene credibly reported unto us, that the persons that keepe the posession of the said castle have and do borne* [burn] *all kinde of tymber in the said castle, and that they sell the leades and iron*'.

From what information they could gather, the commissioners estimated that it would cost at least £2,000 to repair the stronghold. Clearly, whilst parts of it were still in occupation, the castle was being progressively stripped of anything of value.

In the early seventeenth century Laugharne Castle and its lordship were the source of constant legal disputes. In 1615, a Special Commission was sent from the Court of the Exchequer to survey the castle. Their report, seen here, records that those within 'refused to open the gate' to the commissioners (Copyright: Public Record Office, E 178/5069).

THE CIVIL WAR

Sir Sackville Crowe conveyed the castle to Sir William Russell who sided with the Royalist faction during the Civil War.

In the early part of 1644, Laugharne appears to have been under Parliamentarian control. In June of that year, Sir Charles Gerard (d. 1694) led a Royalist army westward through south Wales and, by the end of that month, the castles at Kidwelly, Carmarthen, Cardigan, Newcastle Emlyn and Laugharne were in his hands. Haverfordwest Castle was blockaded and Major-General Rowland Laugharne's troops withdrew into the last two surviving Parliamentarian strongholds of Tenby and Pembroke. Meanwhile, events in England had undergone a sudden change with the defeat of the king's army on 2 July at the battle of Marston Moor. Three weeks later Gerard removed his army to England, leaving troops only to maintain the blockade of Haverfordwest and scattered garrisons in the castles he had captured. One such garrison, that at Laugharne Castle, was

A portrait of the Royalist commander, Sir Charles Gerard (d. 1694), by William Dobson. Gerard captured a string of castles across south Wales on behalf of the king in the early part of 1644. One of those was Laugharne, where he left a Royalist garrison on his return to England in July (By kind permission of Dunedin Public Art Gallery, New Zealand).

THE SEIGE OF LAUGHARNE CASTLE

On the night of Monday 28 October 1644, Major-General Rowland Laugharne's Parliamentarian troops were camped to the north and within a mile of Laugharne Castle (A on map). The next morning Laugharne moved his troops to the area of Glan-y-môr, overlooking the castle from the north-east (B), from whence he began a cannon bombardment. When this 'softening up' failed to bring about the castle's surrender, 200 musketeers captured the town and the Parliamentarian guns were moved to Fern Hill (C) to the west of the castle from where they opened fire on the outer gatehouse. Still the Royalists held out.

On Wednesday night, Laugharne's troops captured the town gate (D) where he mounted guns which were able to fire directly at the front of the outer gatehouse of the castle. The bombardment lasted throughout Thursday and Friday.

Finally, at 11 o'clock on Saturday night, in good clear weather, 200 chosen men made a

Two cannon balls from the demi-culverin used during the Parliamentarian siege of the castle in 1644. They were found embedded in the masonry of the outer gatehouse.

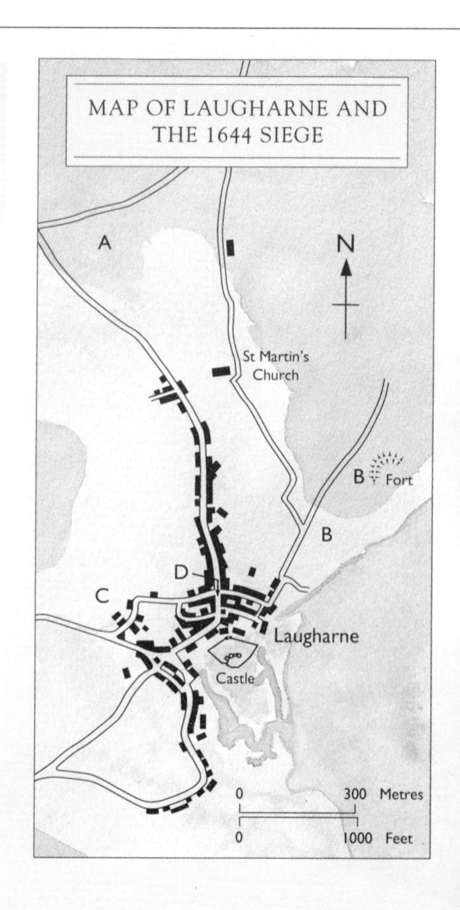

described by the Parliamentarians as 'one of the holds from whence our forces and the country received the greatest annoyance'.

Reinforced by troops from England, and equipped with a powerful demi-culverin ship's gun, on 28 October Major-General Rowland Laugharne assembled an army of about 2,000 men at a point about two miles (3.2km) from Laugharne Castle. After a week-long siege, culminating in a night-time attack, the garrison of some 200 men surrendered under the command of Lieutenant-Colonel Sir William Russell. The officers were allowed to march away, most of them joining the next Royalist garrison at Carmarthen.

Either shortly after the siege, or some time later in the Civil War, parts of the castle were deliberately demolished so that it could no longer serve as a stronghold. This and the cannonfire accounts for the ruined front of the outer gatehouse and the missing eastern side of the inner ward and north-eastern curtain of the outer ward.

Major-General Rowland Laugharne who led the Parliamentary force of some 2,000 men which besieged Laugharne Castle from 28 October to 3 November, 1644. An illustration from England's Worthies, *by John Vicars, London 1647 (By kind permission of the British Library).*

frontal attack on the outer gate of the castle which was captured after a short but fierce fight. About two hours later the defenders called out of the windows of the inner ward for a parley. At 7 o'clock on the morning of Sunday, 3 November, the Royalist garrison surrendered.

The Parliamentarians lost about ten men in the engagement with another thirty or so wounded. Thirty-three of the defenders were killed and an unspecified number wounded.

Left: *This back plate, probably from a pikeman's armour, was found in the post-Civil War demolition deposits at the castle.*

Below: *Typically, the pikeman's armour covered his torso and thighs. His helmet or 'pot' was very simple. This assemblage gives some impression of those pieces which would have been worn with the Laugharne back plate (By courtesy of the Board of Trustees of the Royal Armouries).*

Left: *The north and north-east faces of the medieval stronghold were vulnerable to cannon bombardment from the rising ground north of the town. The ancient earthwork at Glan-y-môr, at the top right of this picture, may have been used by the Parliamentarians as a battery position.*

An engraving of Laugharne Castle published in 1740 by the brothers Samuel and Nathaniel Buck (By courtesy of the National Library of Wales).

LATER HISTORY

The castle, now in ruins, was later restored to Sir William Russell who subsequently sold it to Sir John Powell. Powell's granddaughter, Mary, sold the castle to Pennoyre Watkins who left it to his granddaughter, Elizabeth Ravenscroft.

At some point in the eighteenth century, the castle grounds appear to have been landscaped. New stretches of garden wall were built and an embanked walk was created along the eastern side of what remained of the outer curtain wall, leading to the great oriel window at the eastern end of the inner ward.

At the end of the century, Elizabeth Ravenscroft's husband, Richard Isaac Starke, set about creating a garden. This led one contemporary writer to comment in 1804 that '...the proprietor has laid out the inner court as a modern garden, and in every respect done his utmost to destroy the character of the ruin towards the water. Not only the area, but even one of the towers, is converted to the purposes of horticulture, and filled with the incongruous ornaments of evergreens and flowering shrubs'.

The present garden evolved during the nineteenth century. Glasshouses were constructed against the northern brick wall and a whole series of cockle-shell paths was created throughout the garden.

The crumbling masonry was a continuing cause of concern and minor work was carried out, from time to time, to prop up and make safe the most dangerous areas. On a larger scale, the north-west tower was restored with the work being completed in 1935.

From 1934 the Starke family rented the castle to Richard Hughes (1900-76), the author of *A High Wind in Jamaica*. Hughes wrote his second novel, *In Hazard* (published in 1938), in the gazebo overlooking the estuary. Dylan Thomas (1914-53) stayed in Castle House for a short period during the Second World War and he too found inspiration in the gazebo, with its fine views out over the estuary. It was here that Thomas wrote his series of short stories in *Portrait of the Artist as a Young Dog*.

The celebrated author and poet, Dylan Thomas (1914-53), found inspiration in the gazebo on the outer curtain wall of the castle. It was here, with views over the estuary, that Thomas wrote his series of short stories, Portrait of the Artist as a Young Dog. *This portrait of the young Thomas is by Augustus John (By permission of the National Museum and Gallery, Cardiff).*

From 1934 onwards, the Starke family rented the castle to the author, Richard Hughes (1900-76). He wrote his second novel, In Hazard, *in the gazebo (By kind permission of members of Richard Hughes's family).*

The castle remained in the ownership of the Starke family until 1973 when Miss Anne Starke placed it in the guardianship of the Secretary of State for Wales. Shortly afterwards, work started on consolidating the masonry and this was accompanied by archaeological excavations which took place each summer between 1976 and 1993. The gardens have been restored with plants all of which would have been found in a Victorian garden. The castle is now maintained by Cadw: Welsh Historic Monuments.

Above: *The overgrown ruins of the castle before the work of conservation began.*

Left: *A general view of the great hall area during one season of the archaeological excavations which took place at Laugharne from 1976 until 1993.*

The magnificent watercolour of Laugharne Castle by J. M. W. Turner (1775-1851). The sketches for the view were made on one of the artist's tours in 1795, though the painting was not finished until 1831 (By courtesy of the Columbus Museum of Art, Ohio, USA).

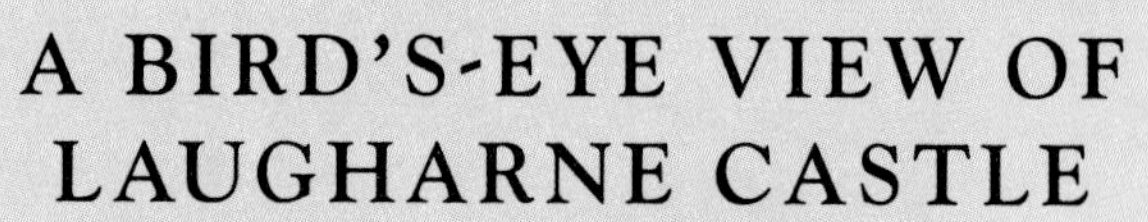

A BIRD'S-EYE VIEW OF LAUGHARNE CASTLE

FROM THE NORTH

14 Gazebo – *This garden summerhouse was built over the base of a medieval tower. The tower was incorporated into the stretch of outer curtain wall which closed off the eastern end of the inner ward ditch (pp. 46, 48).*

13 Eastern and South-Eastern Ranges – *These ranges of Tudor buildings were similar in appearance to the surviving northern range. They were damaged during the Civil War siege and subsequently dismantled, rendering the castle defenceless (pp. 38-40).*

12 South-East Tower – *This angular tower with the adjoining ground-floor postern entrance was added in the middle of the fourteenth century (p. 40).*

11 Great Hall – *This area was occupied by a first-floor hall in both the medieval and Tudor periods. The opening for a Tudor oriel window at the upper end of the hall still survives (pp. 41-3).*

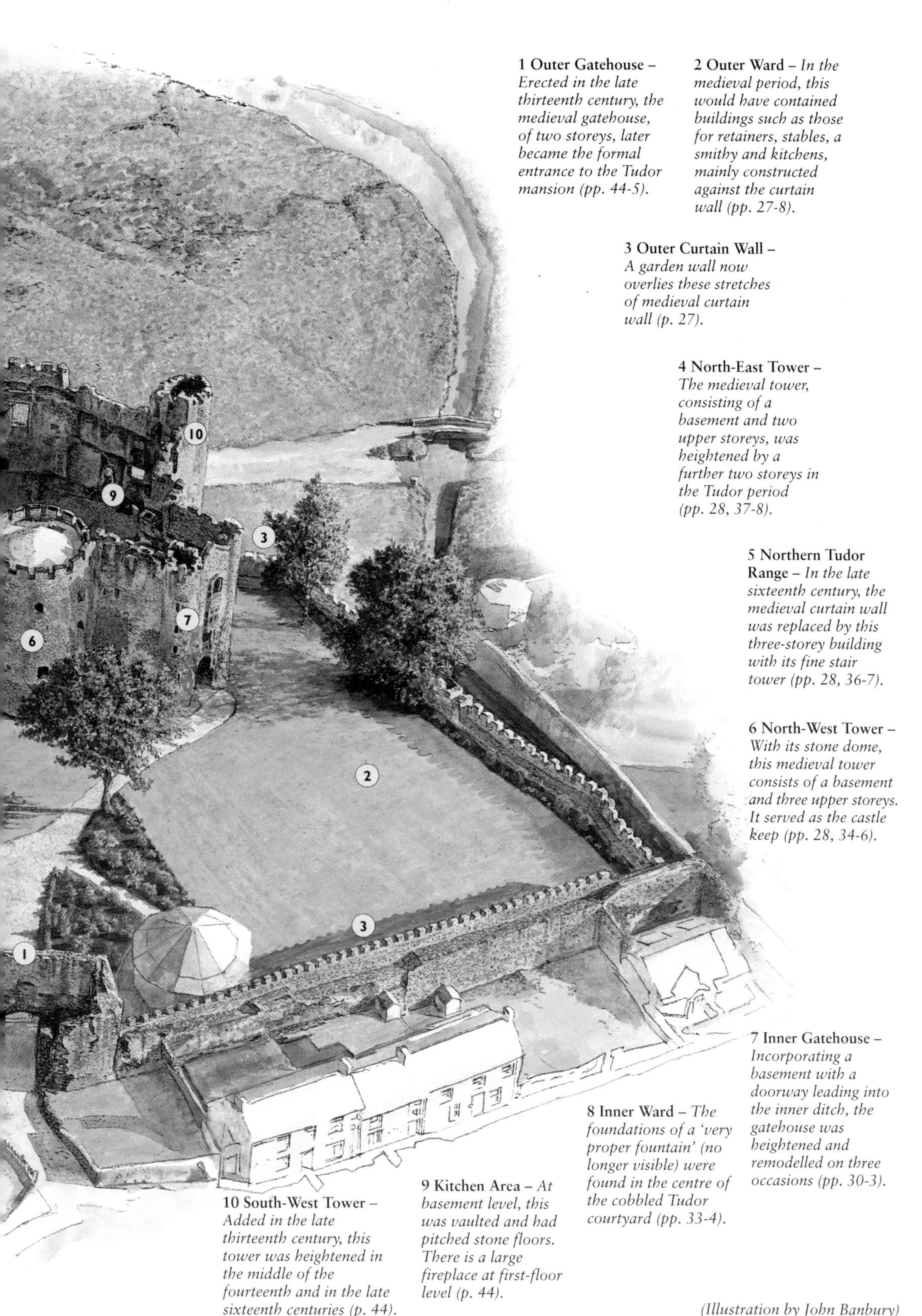

1 Outer Gatehouse – *Erected in the late thirteenth century, the medieval gatehouse, of two storeys, later became the formal entrance to the Tudor mansion (pp. 44-5).*

2 Outer Ward – *In the medieval period, this would have contained buildings such as those for retainers, stables, a smithy and kitchens, mainly constructed against the curtain wall (pp. 27-8).*

3 Outer Curtain Wall – *A garden wall now overlies these stretches of medieval curtain wall (p. 27).*

4 North-East Tower – *The medieval tower, consisting of a basement and two upper storeys, was heightened by a further two storeys in the Tudor period (pp. 28, 37-8).*

5 Northern Tudor Range – *In the late sixteenth century, the medieval curtain wall was replaced by this three-storey building with its fine stair tower (pp. 28, 36-7).*

6 North-West Tower – *With its stone dome, this medieval tower consists of a basement and three upper storeys. It served as the castle keep (pp. 28, 34-6).*

7 Inner Gatehouse – *Incorporating a basement with a doorway leading into the inner ditch, the gatehouse was heightened and remodelled on three occasions (pp. 30-3).*

8 Inner Ward – *The foundations of a 'very proper fountain' (no longer visible) were found in the centre of the cobbled Tudor courtyard (pp. 33-4).*

9 Kitchen Area – *At basement level, this was vaulted and had pitched stone floors. There is a large fireplace at first-floor level (p. 44).*

10 South-West Tower – *Added in the late thirteenth century, this tower was heightened in the middle of the fourteenth and in the late sixteenth centuries (p. 44).*

(Illustration by John Banbury)

A TOUR OF THE CASTLE

Having entered the castle through the outer gatehouse, and upon leaving the visitor centre, this tour begins with a description of the outer ward. It is worth taking the time to get your bearings before proceeding. From the outer ward, the tour progresses to the inner gatehouse and then on to the inner courtyard. The buildings of the inner ward are described in a clockwise order, beginning with the north-west tower. On leaving the castle, you may wish to look at the details of the outer gatehouse. Finally, there is a description of the southern face of the castle viewed from the foreshore below.

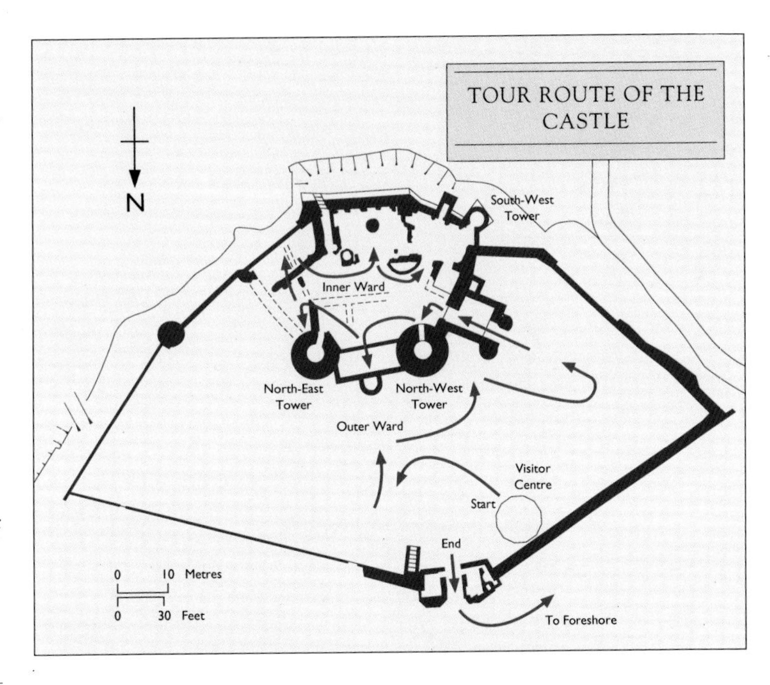

THE OUTER WARD

Just outside the visitor centre, you will find yourself standing in the outer ward. Directly ahead of you is the northern face of the inner ward.

The first point to note is that the ground level to the right, with its lawned surface, bears no resemblance to the medieval topography. When the Norman castle was sited here in the early twelfth century, the ground sloped steeply away. It ran down to the small River Coran which still flows just below the present western wall of the outer enclosure. Something of this original slope can still be appreciated in Wogan Street, the town's main road, immediately outside the castle entrance.

Left: *A general view of the inner ward of the castle, looking west.*

On the far side of the lawn, the bottom of the Norman ringwork ditch was found during excavation. It lay some 23 feet (7m) below the present ground surface. With each successive period in the development of the medieval castle, the ground level was raised, reaching its present height when the garden was created in the later eighteenth century.

It was Guy de Brian V who gave the outer ward its present shape with the construction of the curtain wall in the late thirteenth century. Today, its alignment is mirrored by a wall with mock battlements built when the castle grounds were turned into a garden in the Georgian period. From outside the castle, to the north-west, south-west, and to the east, it is still possible to see the medieval walls underlying the later work.

In fact, there is only one short stretch of medieval curtain wall still standing to its full height. To see this, you should turn to face the outer gatehouse, and look to the right. The surviving section extends from the gate itself to the more recent brick wall which now forms the north-eastern boundary of the castle grounds.

Still facing north, you should next appreciate that beyond the outer curtain wall, the castle was further protected by an outer ditch. The eastern end of this ditch (to your far right) was located during the excavation of the castle. It was found to lie just inside the north-eastern corner of the garden, and from there extended westwards beneath the line of the later brick wall, and on across the face of the outer gatehouse. Towards the north-eastern corner, then, the medieval curtain wall must have extended further into the garden than its brick successor.

Indeed, excavations in this same corner not only located the inner edge of the castle ditch, along with the original line of the curtain wall, but also revealed the remains of a short stretch of clay bank. The bank was probably part of the defences of the earliest Norman ringwork castle. In turn, this suggests that the position of the ditch remained unchanged throughout the castle's history, at least in this area.

The area of the outer ward to the east of the outer gatehouse would have always been fairly narrow, squeezed as it was between the outer curtain wall and the ditch encircling the northern side of the inner ward. Nevertheless, it is possible to imagine medieval buildings similar to those found in the excavations on the western side of the outer ward. There, in the now lawned area once again, buildings were found to be constructed against the inner face of the curtain wall. These might have included accommodation for retainers, stables, a smithy, kitchens, a brewhouse, and so on.

By the late sixteenth century, the area of the outer ward was occupied by an outer court. There was a separate garden covering about an acre (0.4ha), lying just outside the castle on the town side.

THE INNER WARD: EXTERIOR

You should now turn and look towards the inner ward. We shall consider the individual buildings in more detail shortly, but we might first consider the detail on this northern face. From the visitor centre, move to the left, and stand somewhere near the large tree.

The area occupied by the inner ward formed the core of the castle and was in continuous use from the early years of the twelfth century right through until its partial dismantlement in the middle of the seventeenth century. It too was encircled, on this northern side, by a ditch. At its eastern (left) end, archaeological excavation revealed that the ditch was 56 feet (17m) wide at its top.

On your far left is the ruined north-east tower [1], and to the right is the better preserved and now battlemented north-west tower [2], both built by Guy de Brian IV around the middle of the thirteenth century. At the time, they were linked by a section of plain curtain wall. The north-west tower, which has a stone-domed roof, must have served as the medieval keep. The upper part was in a very ruinous condition until it was restored in the early 1930s. The battlements [3] and present window openings (some of which may replace Tudor predecessors) all date to that restoration. On the face of the tower, it is still possible to see medieval arrowslits [4] which were blocked up and rendered over when the castle was converted into a Tudor mansion.

The ruinous north-east tower was heightened in the late sixteenth century. It was at this time that the thirteenth-century curtain wall between the two towers was completely taken down and replaced by the range of buildings which now lies in front of you [5]. The most prominent feature in this northern range is the tall and very elegant stair tower which projects forward [6]. It is easily recognized with its square-headed Tudor windows at all levels.

From here, you should now turn to the right and walk towards the entrance to the inner ward.

Right: *The exterior of the northern face of the inner ward. The numbers highlight features described in the text.*

3
6
2
4
5

We will begin by looking at the external detail of this inner gatehouse. An imposing feature of several phases, it initially took shape in the late thirteenth century. It formed part of the second stage of works undertaken by the de Brian family.

To begin with, the gate consisted of just an entrance passage with one floor above. Look for the surviving redder masonry of this first gateway in the lower part of the north (left) face. Near the top of this early masonry, less than half-way up the side wall of the gatehouse, you will see a line of blocked-up arrowslits. Below the arrowslits there is a row of large square holes, which once extended right through the masonry. These holes may have held timbers supporting an external wooden fighting platform or *hourd*. Although this may seem to be at a rather low level, you must bear in mind that in the medieval period the point where you are now standing would have been a deep ditch.

Less than half-way up the side of the north face of the inner gatehouse, there are traces of blocked-up arrowslits and holes which once may have supported the timbers of a wooden fighting platform.

The gatehouse was raised by a further storey around the middle of the fourteenth century, and was heightened yet again in the late sixteenth century.

The best position from which to examine the façade of the gatehouse is to stand back near the far side of the lawn. Today, you obtain a fine view of the building as it would have appeared in the late sixteenth century when it served as the formal entrance to Sir John Perrot's mansion. From archaeological excavation, we know that the ditch encircling the inner ward still existed in the late sixteenth century. Access to the gateway must, as in earlier periods, have been by way of a wooden bridge.

To the right of the gatehouse, you will observe three quite different types of masonry in the inner curtain wall. At the lowest level, rising to about the same height as the now battlemented outer garden wall, and including a blocked arrowslit, the wall is built of a mixture of red and green stone. This would seem to represent the first de Brian family works in the mid thirteenth century. Above this, there is a large area of unmixed green stone. Both here, and where it appears elsewhere in the castle, this masonry is characteristic of the final de Brian work, dating to the middle years of the fourteenth century. Finally, the upper masonry belongs to the Perrot period in the late sixteenth century.

INNER GATEHOUSE

The rather eccentric late thirteenth-century ground plan of the inner gatehouse remained unaltered throughout the castle's history. And this despite progressive heightening and modifications to the façade.

You should now proceed into the gate-passage and pause on the modern wooden bridge. Look down into the area beneath the bridge, and you will see a large doorway deep beneath the entrance. This was discovered during the excavations. The clue to what has happened within the gatehouse lies in the sunken nature of the Tudor cobbled surface.

From the plan at the back of this guide, you can trace the position of the earliest de Brian gate. It was a simple break in the curtain wall with a ditch outside.

The sloping face of the mid thirteenth-century inner curtain wall can still be traced near the back of the gatehouse, as a butt joint in the masonry.

It is still possible to see the sloping face of the wall of this period. It is especially clear near the back of the gatehouse, to the left of the modern bridge, where it appears as a butt joint in the masonry. Opposite this, the same sloping face can be seen on the inner face of a later latrine pit on the other side of the gatehouse.

In the late thirteenth century, Guy de Brian V transformed this simple entrance by building a gatehouse out over the earlier defensive ditch. The masons took the opportunity to create a basement below the main entrance passage. At the front of the basement, a small doorway, known as a postern, led out from the gate.

Right: *The gatehouse into the inner ward. It was added in the later thirteenth century, heightened in the mid fourteenth century, and transformed in the Elizabethan period.*

This iron key may have been used to lock the postern door located in the basement beneath the gatehouse. It was found during the excavations.

This ingenious little feature gave access to a pathway along the inner edge of a new defensive ditch, and on to a further doorway which led out through the outer curtain wall to the foreshore below (p. 46). An iron key, perhaps used to lock the postern door, was found during the excavations on the floor of the basement.

As constructed, the basement extended under the entire area of the gatehouse. However, during the archaeological work, it was decided to excavate just a small section where the later Tudor cobbled surface had been destroyed. Hence you will find a revetment wall retaining the unexcavated area below the modern bridge. In the late thirteenth century, the floor over the basement was of wood. You will see three of the stone corbels which supported the main beams of this floor near the foot of the southern wall (right of the bridge).

The basement was eventually filled in when the gatehouse was heightened in the middle of the fourteenth century.

The last feature to note before leaving the interior of the gatehouse is the position of the entrance passage. This is more or less represented by the modern bridge, lying as it does on the

The details of the inner gatehouse viewed from the courtyard. The numbers highlight those features described in the tour text.

northern side. On the left, there are two embrasures for arrowslits surviving in the lower wall. To the right, there must have been a substantial wooden partition closing off the passage from a guardchamber beyond. This chamber had a fireplace which is now blocked, though you will see its side dressings near the outer (right) side of the gate.

In the Tudor period, this earlier medieval arrangement was considerably modified. The ground floor into Sir John Perrot's mansion was one open area with a fine cobbled surface throughout.

You should now continue through to the courtyard and look back at the upper details of the gatehouse. From this position, it is possible to trace the sequence of development. As we have seen, the late thirteenth-century arrangement comprised a basement, a ground floor with the entrance passage, and a first floor above. The wall-walk level in this period is indicated by an offset [**1**] on either side of the gatehouse. From this point, a thinner parapet wall would have extended upwards.

In the time of Guy de Brian VII, about the middle of the fourteenth century, the gatehouse was raised by another storey. This can again be detected by the higher offset on the left-hand side [**2**].

The dressed capital which survives in the north-west corner in the upper room of the gatehouse.

Once more, the offset represents the wall-walk level in this period. There is a fine dressed capital in the upper right-hand corner of the upper room [**3**]. It is possible that this second-floor chamber served as a chapel in both the medieval and Tudor periods, with the altar at the east end overlooking the courtyard.

Also from this mid fourteenth-century period, notice on the left, near the inner side, a series of latrine chutes at this corner of the gatehouse [**4**]. The chutes extend down to a pit which discharged through the gatehouse wall and out into the ditch.

At the time of Sir John Perrot, in the late sixteenth century, the gatehouse saw two more phases of alteration. Look to the far end, and evidence for the first work can be seen in the large blocked window [**5**] with the distinctive gabled roof creasing high above [**6**]. Subsequently, the gatehouse was raised with the top of the roof at the present upper gable level [**7**].

A doorway at first-floor level in the far right-hand corner [**8**] (north-west) leads into a rounded tower. This contains a staircase providing access to the upper floors of the gate and to latrine chambers at each floor level.

Finally, it seems that the back of the gatehouse was always constructed of timber, from first-floor level upwards.

INNER COURTYARD

Today, one gains a false impression of space within the castle's inner ward. From the thirteenth century onwards, it was enclosed on all sides by high walls and would have seemed much smaller than is conveyed by its current open aspect. The two great towers would then, as now, have dominated the northern side of the courtyard, on your left. To your immediate right, in the south-west corner, would have been the castle kitchens. Adjacent to the kitchens was the Tudor great hall with its large oriel window, occupying the same position as the medieval hall. Further ranges of rooms stretch around the eastern side of the ward, and together all these buildings enclosed a space described in the 1592 survey (p. 39) as *'a little Inner court of ffowerscore and tenn yards compass'*.

Above: *Small patches of the original Tudor cobbling survive in the inner ward, surrounded by modern cobbles.*

Right: *Lead musket balls from the Civil War attack were found amongst the courtyard cobbles during the archaeological excavations.*

At the time of the 1592 survey, the surface of the inner courtyard was cobbled. Small patches of the Tudor cobbling, similar to that in the gatehouse, still survive surrounded by modern cobbles. Lead musket balls from the Civil War attack were found amongst these cobbles during the archaeological excavations.
In the middle of the courtyard, the excavations also revealed the footings of the Tudor *'very proper fountaine'* (p. 39).

Evidence was also found of the lead water pipes which fed the fountain. There is a reference in an inventory of the castle, also dating to 1592, to 'a fountayne in and about which is of lead by estymacion c. wzt. [one hundredweight]', valued at four shillings.

Ahead, the modern stone-flagged path has been set out in deliberate fashion. The grassed area to the left marks the general location of the twelfth-century stone, Norman hall block. The path lies on the line of its southern wall, and has been constructed to the same width. A fragment of the eastern wall of the hall block can be seen at the far end, disappearing beneath the later round, north-east tower. Only the eastern part of the hall block was fully excavated, though a partition wall was found. This has been marked out, with edging stones, in the lawn.

NORTH-WEST TOWER OR KEEP

The north-west tower was built around the middle of the thirteenth century by Guy de Brian IV. It consists of a basement with three upper storeys.

In the medieval period, the tower was entered at first-floor level via an external flight of wooden stairs from the courtyard. The entrance continued as stone steps, through the thickness of the masonry, to the interior of the tower. The sides of the lower part of the doorway can be seen as straight joints in the external masonry. They are situated below the later Tudor window which in turn replaced the original door.

In the Tudor period, a new entrance was cut through the ground-floor level of the tower, giving access to the basement.

The medieval entrance into the north-west tower was at first-floor level. The doorway was blocked in the Tudor period.

A doorway in the left-hand side of this entrance (obscured by later repairs) led to a new flight of stairs. These led up to the first-floor room of the tower. The basement itself, which appears to have had no windows, was subsequently converted into a wine cellar. The Tudor blocking of the trapdoor, through which the basement was entered in the medieval period, can be clearly seen in the centre of the ceiling of this room.

Today, a modern wooden staircase leads up into the tower. You pass through what would have been a solid screen wall in the Tudor period. At that time, a flight of stairs led up to a lobby where access could be gained to a Tudor staircase turret. The turret was tucked into the angle between the tower and the gatehouse.

Turn right at the top of the modern stairs, and pass into the first of the three upper rooms of the tower.

This tower was the castle's principal stronghold and, as can be seen on this, and the two floors above, it was a formidable fighting machine with arrowslits facing in every direction. Furthermore, stone floors at first- and second-floor levels, and a fine stone-vaulted roof, made the tower more or less fireproof.

A stair, just next to the blocked thirteenth-century first-floor entrance, leads up to the second floor. Near the top of this flight of steps, a doorway with a modern blocking on the left, led to the Tudor stair turret.

A cutaway reconstruction of the inner gatehouse, the north-west tower, and the northern Tudor range, viewed from the south. The illustration shows the arrangements in these areas in the late sixteenth century (Illustration by Chris Jones-Jenkins, 1995).

The inner curving face of the north-west tower can still be seen at second-floor level, despite the Tudor alterations at this point.

The second-floor chamber was originally divided from that above by the tower's one wooden floor. In the Tudor period these two rooms were merged by the removal of the floor. At the same time, a massive stone arch was inserted into the east wall, and this meant the upper room of the contemporary northern range extended into the earlier tower. It would have created a single long apsidal-ended chamber. The present wall beneath the arch, along with the rather crude window openings, were all added as part of the repairs in the 1930s. Look down at the floor of this room, and you will easily distinguish the original inner curving face of the tower.

Two twelfth-century, bone gaming pieces found during excavations at the castle. That on the right was later reused as a spindlewhorl.

The north-west tower was built as part of Guy de Brian IV's works in the middle of the thirteenth century. It must have served as the castle keep.

The upper room contained the only concession to any form of comfort with a small fireplace. The tower is without any sanitary provision in the form of latrines.

The next flight of stairs leads to the level of the thirteenth-century upper room. It is now no more than a landing, sitting on top of a concrete ring beam inserted as part of the earlier repairs to this tower. The concrete stairs by which you have climbed to the room also date to the earlier phase of restoration. From the landing, you are able to appreciate the quality of the stone dome. This can only be matched by that at the top of William Marshal's (d. 1219) great stone *donjon* at Pembroke Castle.

The final flight of steps leads to the battlement level, which is again a feature of the 1930s restoration. It is well worth taking the time to climb to the top to observe the surrounding views.

The fine stone dome which forms the roof of the north-west tower. Its quality can only be matched by a larger dome at Pembroke Castle.

The southern face of the northern Tudor range. There are two large blocked windows at each of the three floor levels.

NORTHERN TUDOR RANGE

Back at ground level, you should next consider the well-preserved range on the northern side of the courtyard. In the medieval period, there was a simple curtain wall at this point, linking the north-west to the north-east round towers. The wall must have been taken down in the late sixteenth century when the present building was constructed.

Standing back in the courtyard and looking at its southern face, you can see two large blocked windows at each of the three floor levels. The blocking dates to the eighteenth or nineteenth centuries. Notice the once fine sandstone dressings still surviving at the heads of the four upper windows. From here, enter the building via the ground-floor doorway.

Opposite the door, there is a semi-circular stair tower which led up to each of the floors above. A trap door in its floor provided access to a basement, best seen from the outside of the tower. Looking up, you can trace the line of the wooden treads of the staircase, lit at every level by a fine series of windows.

A general view, looking east, within the northern Tudor range. There is evidence for two phases of roof against the gable wall.

The north-east tower was first built at the time of Guy de Brian IV. It was raised by a further two storeys in the late sixteenth century.

The long second-floor room was the only chamber in the northern range to be provided with a fireplace. Before the side of the adjacent north-west tower was refaced in the 1930s, this fairly grand rectangular space was extended into the body of the circular tower. It would have created one large chamber of somewhat unusual form.

As we observed with the inner gatehouse, there appear to have been two phases of late sixteenth-century roof over the northern range. Sir John Perrot's original roof was of a low pitch, and was probably covered with lead. The roof level was accessible from the uppermost doorway of the stair tower. Look high up from the centre of the range and you will see the doorway has stone jambs, reflecting the fact that it was designed as an external feature exposed to the weather. The line of the earlier roof can be seen against the gable wall at the eastern end of the building. Not long after its construction, the range was raised in height and an attic was inserted. A window at the eastern end can be seen below the creasing of this new pitched roof. This creasing extended along both the south and north walls at battlement level.

NORTH-EAST TOWER

Back in the courtyard, turn to the left to examine the thirteenth-century north-east tower. As built by Guy de Brian IV, this was not as high as its north-western counterpart. There were just two upper floors over a basement. The basement was entered at ground-floor level by a doorway from the courtyard. The tower was then raised by a further two storeys in the late sixteenth century.

Stand and look at the tower from the courtyard side. To the left, its western side had to be refaced when the inner wall of the eastern (right-hand) Tudor range was constructed. The range itself has now disappeared which makes this a little difficult to appreciate. In the same phase of remodelling, the medieval masonry on the southern face of the tower was cut back to create a staircase. This can still be seen extending to the top of the tower.

The interior of the tower is best viewed from its now-ruined eastern side (around to the right). The first floor had three embrasures for arrowslits which were subsequently altered. That on the east, as a result of later medieval modifications, became a doorway leading to a latrine chamber contrived in the thickness of the wall. The latrine chute can still be seen on the outer face of the tower. The western embrasure was converted into a doorway leading into the first floor of the northern Tudor range. At the same time, the embrasure to the north became a window.

At second-floor level, one of the surviving embrasures was later converted into a fireplace. A doorway on the south-east side led out on to the wall-walk of the medieval east curtain.

Another doorway on the south-west led to a stair contrived in the thickness of the wall. This rose to the medieval wall-walk level, which is itself now represented by a wide ledge. On this, two further storeys were constructed in the Tudor period. At that time, there was no longer a need for defensive strength, and a much thinner outer wall could be employed. This created larger rooms than those in the earlier medieval tower below.

EASTERN RANGE

The range along the eastern side of the courtyard takes more effort to reconstruct. Its various phases are represented by little more than fragments of foundation, together with scars left against the adjacent north-east tower. It was this side, together with the area to the south-east, which was probably destroyed by a combination of cannonfire during the Civil War siege and subsequent dismantlement.

In the late twelfth century, the eastern end of the inner ward was defended by a Norman bank. The hall block, the south wall of which is now represented by the slabbed path, was built into the rear of this bank. From the south-east corner of the hall block, a wall extended right through to the cliff edge (see the plan at the back of this guide). A small piece of the footings of this wall survives above ground.

In the mid thirteenth century, the Norman hall-block was demolished and the level of the inner ward raised with made-up ground during the works of Guy de Brian IV. His new eastern curtain wall extended from the contemporary north-east tower to the south-eastern corner of the inner ward. Again, the alignment of the curtain wall in this period shows on the plan at the back of the guide.

You will still see a fragment of the lowermost part of Guy IV's rounded turret in the south-east corner. The northern end of the eastern curtain wall appears as a stub of masonry at the base of the north-east tower. The toothing where it joined the tower can be seen above.

Notice that the foundations of the tower at this point run over the north-eastern corner of the twelfth-century hall block. They are in fact higher than the present ground surface. This is because the original thirteenth-century ground level was completely cut away by the insertion of the later Tudor buildings.

The line of the mid thirteenth-century curtain wall along the eastern side of the inner ward has all but disappeared. In this view, the toothing where it joined the north-east tower can still be seen.

This is an important point, and there is evidence for the same reduction of levels throughout the inner ward. It means that the late sixteenth-century surfaces lie immediately on top of twelfth-century levels. Unfortunately, apart from the lower part of foundations, archaeological evidence for occupation of the inner ward during the thirteenth century has almost completely disappeared.

When Sir John Perrot's builders came to build a new range along the eastern side of the inner ward, they reused the thirteenth-century curtain as the outer wall. This Tudor range may have resembled that on the northern side of the courtyard.

Traces of Guy de Brian IV's rounded turret in the south-east corner of the inner ward can be seen in this view. The eastern curtain wall extended along a line from here to the north-east tower.

Excavation revealed that the Tudor floor had been resurfaced at least once. A passage from the central courtyard provided access to the ground-floor rooms. An external stair (no longer visible) in the south-eastern corner of the inner courtyard led up to the first-floor level.

SOUTH-EASTERN RANGE

Overlooking the coast, on this side of the courtyard, are the low foundations of the south-eastern range. The visible footings are of two periods. As elsewhere, the thirteenth-century floor surfaces were cut away in the late sixteenth century. At that time, the plaster floors of the rooms extended over the earlier footings, abutting thinner Tudor walls which have now disappeared. The full height of this range in the late sixteenth century can be appreciated from the short length of wall extending out from the eastern side of the angular south-east tower, which lies to the right.

A SURVEY OF 1592

A Booke of Survey of the Castle, Lordship, and Manor of Tallaugharne, alias Laugharne, the Second Day of October, in the XXXIIIth Yeare of the Raigne of our Soveraigne Lady Elizabeth

A survey of Laugharne was taken in 1592, at the time of Sir John Perrot's conviction for treason. The detail it provides on the condition of the castle is of considerable interest:

'The same is situate upon ye South Side of the Towne of Laugharne, and adjoining to ye same, the chiefe prospectes whereof are toward a creek that floweth from Seavern close to ye said castle, and III miles higher into ye land. At ye entry whereof from ye said towne is a faire gatehouse, having in it two lodgings from wch goeth a wall eastward along ye garden after mentioned, compasswise to ye pyle itself, and from ye other side of ye gatehouse westward the like wall, wthn wch court is an outer court of ffower hundred and three yards compass.

The castle or pyle itself, hath at ye entrance into it a strong new gate, over wch are faire chambers wth lights of ffree stone hewed, toward ye sd outer court, the whole building of wch castle is contrived compasswyse from the sd entrance, about a little Inner court of ffowerscore and tenn yards compass; in the middest whereof is a very proper fountaine, wth a stately round stairs of hard lymestone wrought, and a porch over a part thereof leading into a faire hall, at ye upper end whereof is a great dyning chamber, And wthin the whole building a great number of lodgings, and offices faire, and fit for such a pyle:

The same hath been a very ancient castle, but utterly decayed till about XIIII years past when Sir John Perrott did reedify the same, and almost fully finished it, but now many of the windowes, as well wthin as wthout, doe moulder away by force of the weather, and badness of the stone. And the whole castle by reason of the bad buildings thereof (without excessive charges) is like wthin few yeares to run to utter ruin again.'

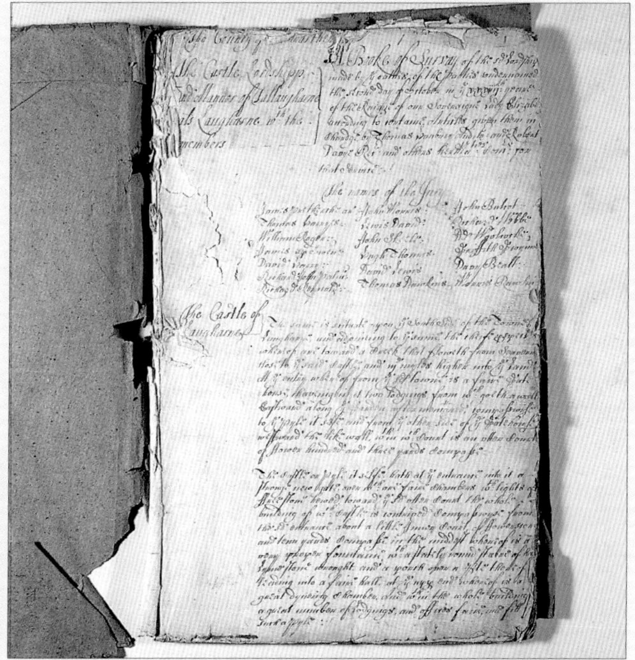

The 1592 survey of the castle and lordship of Laugharne (By courtesy of Laugharne Corporation and Carmarthenshire Record Office, Laugharne 211).

The dimensions of the range closely accord with the description of the dining chamber given in an inventory made at the time of Sir John Perrot's attainder. The dining chamber, which would have been on the first floor, is also referred to in the 1592 survey as being located at the upper end of the great hall. We also learn from the inventory that the room had wooden panelling and contained two tables, each measuring two yards (1.83m), and a livery cupboard.

The room beneath it, on the ground floor, was in use as a store for more wooden panelling which awaited finishing and mounting. The evidence would seem to reinforce the statement in the survey (p. 39) that Perrot's work at Laugharne was not quite complete at the time of his death.

A general view of the south-eastern corner of the inner ward. The view shows the south-east tower, with the low remains of the south-eastern range to the left.

SOUTH-EAST TOWER

This tower was built as part of Guy de Brian VII's works in the mid fourteenth century. It was constructed against the earlier thirteenth-century curtain. Orientate yourself at this point by the small postern gateway which led out to the foreshore.

On the other side of the postern, to the right, the junction between the new masonry and the curtain wall to the west shows up as a straight joint. This can be seen immediately beneath the later oriel window. All of the masonry in the tower itself is of Guy VII's time, except for the uppermost part. This, along with the creasing for the pitched roof, dates to the late sixteenth century. As elsewhere, all the present window openings are also of Tudor date.

The postern doorway probably replaced that in the basement of the inner gatehouse (pp. 30, 32). It was under Guy VII that the gatehouse postern was blocked and the basement filled in. The grooves at either side of this fourteenth-century postern entrance may have been for a portcullis, despite not being directly opposite one another. The insertion of the Tudor oriel window above would have rendered such a portcullis redundant. A fine stone-slabbed Tudor drain, found during the excavations, ran from the eastern range, across the courtyard, and down the postern passage. It led out of the castle beneath the steps leading down through the postern. In the second Tudor phase the postern was blocked up. It has been reopened as part of the modern conservation works.

In the sides of the postern doorway below the south-east tower there are grooves which may have been for a portcullis.

The great hall was the centre of administrative and social life in the medieval castle. This late thirteenth-century manuscript illustration shows a lord, his wife, and guests, dining in a great hall (By kind permission of the British Library, Additional Ms. 28162, f. 10v).

GREAT HALL

The straight stretch of curtain wall along the southern side of the inner ward always seems to have formed the outer wall of the great hall. This was the centre of administrative and social life within the castle. There was a hall here serving all the de Brian lords from Guy IV onwards. It saw further extensive modifications when the castle was remodelled as Sir John Perrot's mansion. From at least the late thirteenth century onwards, the hall was situated at first-floor level, raised over a sub-basement. The structural sequence is quite complex, and is most easily understood by starting with the latest Tudor arrangements. and working backwards in time.

HISTORICAL SUMMARY AND THE CASTLE BUILDING SEQUENCE

First Ringwork and Ringwork with Rectangular Hall Block

- 1116: 'And to Bleddyn ap Cedifor was entrusted the castle of Robert Courtemain which was at Abercorram'. The first ringwork phase of the castle.
- 1172: Parley between Henry II (1154-89) and Rhys ap Gruffudd (d.1197) at Laugharne.
- 1189: Rhys ap Gruffudd captures the castles of St Clears, Abercorram and Llansteffan.
- 1215: The forces of Llywelyn ab Iorwerth (d. 1240) 'overthrew to the ground Llansteffan and St Clears and Laugharne'.

The First De Brian Castle

- 1247: Grant to Guy de Brian IV and his heirs of a yearly fair at his manor of Talachar.
- 1257: The Welsh 'burned the castle of Abercorram and Llansteffan and Arberth [Narberth] … and Maenclochog and all the towns that adjoined them'.
- 1258: Having been captured by the Welsh, Guy de Brian is released upon payment of a ransom.

Castle Defences Strengthened

- About 1268: Guy de Brian IV dies.
- 1277: Guy de Brian V called to arms by the king.
- 1307: Guy de Brian V dies.

Castle Modernized

- 1330: By about this date, Guy de Brian VI had become feeble and incapable and his son (later Guy de Brian VII) took over control of his father's estates.
- 1349: Guy de Brian VI dies.
- 1370: Guy de Brian VII becomes the 56th member of the Order of the Garter.
- 1390: Guy de Brian VII dies and the male line fails.

Tudor Mansion

- 1575: Queen Elizabeth I grants the Lordship and Castle of Laugharne to Sir John Perrot. He begins to transform the castle into a Tudor mansion.
- 1584: Sir John Perrot's tenancy is confirmed and his building programme may have been extended.
- 1592: Sir John Perrot dies.

Sir John Perrot's Hall

Standing in the middle of the courtyard, you will see that the southern curtain wall has four distinctive features, all dating to the late sixteenth century. On the left is the great oriel window [1] which would have lit the upper end of Sir John Perrot's hall. Midway along the wall is the fireplace, or rather the large hole where the fireplace would have been [2]. What must have been a fine dressed stone surround has long since disappeared. At the right-hand (west) end of the hall is another large window [3]. A line of projecting stone corbels [4], dating to the medieval period, would have supported the floor timbers. The fourth element consists of the mock battlements [5] below which the line of the original roof can be traced, rising to cover small garret rooms. All these features have been inserted into, or added to, the pre-existing medieval wall. The masonry surrounding the Tudor windows and fireplace, and that in the area of the flue above the fireplace, contrasts with the more general red masonry of the medieval centuries.

The wall on the courtyard side of the building was identified through excavation. It survived as a pitched stone footing dating back to the middle of the thirteenth century [6]. The line of this wall is now marked by stone edgings in the present ground surface.The formal approach to Sir John Perrot's hall from the courtyard was via a semi-circular stair [7]. The foundation of the stair can be seen at the western end (right) of the hall. It was described in the 1592 survey as '*a stately round stairs of hard lymestone wrought, and a porch over a part thereof leading into a faire hall*'.

There was a ground-floor doorway on the eastern side of the stair, and this led into the sub-basement below the hall. A stone stairbase, with the slots for a timber staircase, can be seen in the far south-west corner of the sub-basement. The staircase gave access from the adjacent kitchen undercroft up to the hall. Still looking towards the coast, the narrow wall which survives as footings at the opposite end of the hall (left) divided the sub-basement from the postern passage [**8**].

As elsewhere in the castle, the Tudor plaster floors were of two periods. The first was associated with a partition extending down the length of the sub-basement dividing it into at least two rooms. This partition was removed in the second Tudor period. Its position is shown by the parallel edging stones set in the present gravel surface. As in the medieval period, the well was contained in a small extension at the north-eastern corner of the hall [**9**].

Within the hall itself, we know from the 1592 inventory that there was a square table and a very long table measuring six yards (5.5m) with four forms or benches.

Above: *This doorway at Kanturk Castle in Ireland is of similar date to Sir John Perrot's work at Laugharne.*

Right: *This decorative panel found in the excavations at Laugharne probably comes from the lower order of a similar doorway, leading into the first-floor hall.*

The great hall and associated features viewed from the northern side of the inner ward. The numbers highlight those features described in the text.

The Medieval Hall

The three de Brian family phases of work are most easily understood by starting with the earliest evidence.

Nothing survives above ground from the initial phase, and all that has been found are the pitched stone footings [**6**] of the inner wall mentioned above. These footings may have extended further west (right) into the kitchen area. This mid thirteenth-century phase of Guy IV is also represented by the short length of wall, also on a pitched stone foundation, which can still be seen extending south from the eastern end of these footings (just to the south of the Tudor semi-circular stair) [**10**]. Another small stretch of contemporary pitched stone foundations in the south-eastern corner of the hall basement is known from excavation.

By the later thirteenth century, the southern curtain wall, which formed one long side of this hall, may have become unstable and in need of replacement. Certainly, a new curtain was constructed along the entire coastal face of the hall. Late thirteenth-century pottery has been found in the construction trench dug to build this wall. Such major works would have entailed dismantling and rebuilding the southern part of the hall block. The sub-basement windows [**11**] (retained in the Perrot phase) may be contemporary with the late thirteenth-century curtain. The new wall would have stood to the height of the present wall-walk.

Finally, in the middle of the fourteenth century, when the south-east tower was added, the first-floor hall was extended further to the left (east). It ran over the new postern passage [**12**]. At the same time, five small stone footings were constructed against the curtain, perhaps as bases for wallposts to give added support to the timbers of the floor above [**13**]. The well was also constructed [**9**].

The circular stone feature in the middle of the hall basement was also built at this time [**14**]. It was reduced to its present level when the Tudor floors were laid. Before this, it may have been a stone column supporting a central hearth in the hall above.

KITCHEN AREA AND SOUTH-WEST TOWER

From at least the late thirteenth century, the western end of the inner ward appears to have served as a kitchen, with associated general storage and working areas.

You should look first at the southern curtain as it extends westwards (right) from the hall. Here, the lower part of the masonry, extending at least as far as the vaulting pier to the right (west) of the doorway into the latrine projection, dates to the middle of the thirteenth century. Above are extensive repairs of eighteenth- or nineteenth-century date, and include two modern stone piers.

This surviving pier was one of those which supported a stone-vaulted basement in the south-west corner of the inner ward.

A general view of the kitchen area and south-west tower. The huge kitchen fireplace stands out at first-floor level.

Looking further to your right (west), the lower section of the wall extending northwards from the oven area, below the later great fireplace, to the inner end of the gatehouse, is also of the same date.

In the late thirteenth century, this entire corner of the castle underwent major modification. The south-west tower, then of two (possibly three) storeys, was added along with a latrine turret. The basement area was also vaulted at that time. You will see the stubs of vaulting piers against the southern curtain wall. These were matched by similar piers along the centre of the floor area, and presumably against the now missing inner, courtyard-facing wall. Only the easternmost central pier survives. The present pitched-stone Tudor floor surface is at approximately the same level as its medieval predecessor. An archaeomagnetic date has shown that the oven in the lower working area at the western end of the kitchen basement was last used sometime between 1460 and 1520.

The whole of this corner of the inner ward was remodelled above first-floor level in the middle of the fourteenth century. This work is characterized by the use of green stone. A further two storeys were added to the south-west tower. The great kitchen fireplace was built at first-floor level, together with the upper masonry in the western end of the range and in the southern curtain extending east up to the change of alignment. Finally, in the late sixteenth century, a fourth floor was added to the south-west tower and topped with mock Tudor battlements.

OUTER GATEHOUSE

The outer gatehouse, by which you now leave the castle, was built in the late thirteenth century. It was refaced in the middle of the fourteenth century. It always consisted of just two storeys. The earliest work is characterized by the use of red stone. As elsewhere in the castle, the green masonry is representative of mid fourteenth-century work.

At the back of the gate, to the right, the present stone stair, leading up to the wall-walk is probably a later addition. It is, however, in approximately the same position as a stone or timber medieval predecessor. A doorway at this corner led from the wall-walk into the upper floor of the gate, with a stone stair next to this rising to the gatehouse wall-walk level.

As you leave the castle, you should note the doorways at the inner end of the gatehouse passage. They lead into the guardchambers. The roofs of the gate-passage and the guardchambers were stone vaulted.

A cutaway reconstruction of the outer gatehouse as it probably appeared in the mid fourteenth century (Illustration by Chris Jones-Jenkins, 1995).

Fragments of a cannon ball were removed from the masonry at this point during consolidation.

The front of the gatehouse was badly damaged by cannonfire during the Civil War siege and then systematically demolished with the inner end of the causeway and outer end of the gatehouse passage being completely dug away. This is the main reason why it is difficult to reconstruct the earlier medieval arrangements.

The late thirteenth-century gate was approached by a wooden bridge, although no evidence for a drawbridge was found during excavations in front of the gatehouse. By the middle of the fourteenth century, the wooden bridge had been replaced by a stone causeway. The entrance to Sir John Perrot's mansion is described in the late sixteenth century as consisting of, '*a faire gatehouse, having in it two lodgings*'.

The medieval arrangements have survived in an unaltered state in the eastern guardchamber (to the right).

The western guardchamber is less well preserved, but a doorway in the west wall provided access to a passage leading to a latrine in the north-west corner of the tower. At the upper level, a similar passage led to a first-floor latrine which can be seen where the inner face of its chute is now missing.

As you leave the gatehouse, you will see a well preserved arrowslit, of cross-oillet type, on the right-hand side. Also notice the original jambs of the entrance on either side of the gateway. These jambs have small triangular or spur stops. Looking back at the front of the gatehouse, you can see that the eastern chamber, now on your left, was roughly rectangular in shape. The front corners are chamfered with triangular angle buttresses. A similar buttress existed on the right. The front wall then extended back at an angle to the western corner. At this point there was originally a latrine turret. The upper face of the wall in this corner is cracked and set back. This is the result of structural damage caused by cannonfire during the Civil War attack.

The outer gatehouse, which was heavily damaged during the Civil War attack on the castle.

EXTERIOR OF THE CASTLE FROM THE FORESHORE

From the entrance, it is possible to reach the foreshore either by walking down Wogan Street to your left or turning right and following Market Lane down to the far end where a path brings you out close to the north-east corner of the outer ward of the castle. This description begins at the little bridge over the Coran.

To the left of the slender south-west tower, three periods are represented in the outer curtain wall. The lower part, to a point just beyond the change in alignment, is all of medieval date. A wide doorway, now blocked, led through to the inner ward ditch, and eventually on in to the postern doorway beneath the entrance passage of the inner gatehouse (pp. 30, 32). In the late sixteenth century, the width of this outer doorway was halved. It is represented by the two straight joints on the left-hand side of the present blocking.

The upper part of the wall, along with the entire height of the stretch extending north-westwards to the next offset, all date to the Georgian garden period. The final stretch, leading up to the north-west corner, was of the same period but had to be rebuilt from the ground upwards during the recent consolidation works.

There are three building phases represented in the south-west tower. The base of the tower, built of red stone with spur buttresses, is all that remains of the late thirteenth-century construction. Above this, the tower was rebuilt and heightened in the middle of the fourteenth century using green stone. The top third of the tower is all of late sixteenth-century date.

The mid fourteenth-century work can be seen extending into the curtain to the east of the tower, up to and including the small blocked window with a cusped head. You will see the window located just above a corbelled out section of masonry. The area of set-back masonry just below this window, and extending west to the latrine projection, is an eighteenth- or nineteenth-century repair.

The once pent-roofed latrine dates to the late thirteenth century. So, too, does the lower part of the curtain wall immediately to the right, together with the masonry in between the latrine and the south-west tower.

The main stretch of the curtain wall, from ground to wall-walk level, extending eastwards from the area of the repair, to a point just to the west (left) of the postern doorway, is also all of late thirteenth-century date. The two large upper window openings and the battlements belong to Sir John Perrot's modifications in the Tudor period. As noted on the inner face, the Tudor masonry surrounding the windows, and in the area below the chimney where the flue has been inserted, consists of smaller stone than the earlier red medieval masonry. The rectangular south-east tower and the postern entrance were added to this corner of the inner ward in the middle of the fourteenth century.

You should now walk to a point just beyond the south-east tower. Here you will see walls at two levels. Apart from a very short stretch of red mid thirteenth-century curtain wall, just to the east of the tower, all of the lower wall, and the upper wall extending eastwards to the gazebo, date to the garden period.

The outer face of the castle viewed from the foreshore to the south-west.

The gazebo is built upon the base of a medieval tower which was incorporated into the stretch of curtain wall which closed off the eastern end of the inner ward ditch.

Much of the curtain wall beyond the gazebo is built of green stone. It includes a blocked doorway which is similar to that previously described at the western end of the inner ward ditch. In this case, the door provided access directly to the outer ward (the level of which has subsequently been raised as part of the garden landscaping). The use of green stone along this stretch indicates that it dates to the mid fourteenth century. It probably replaced a length of late thirteenth-century curtain. The doorway and walling in the north-east corner date to the garden period. The door provided access from the castle to a small garden area on the terrace between it and the gazebo.

The gazebo on the south-eastern curtain wall. It was built upon the base of a medieval tower. At this point, the curtain wall closed off the eastern end of the inner ward ditch.

FURTHER READING

J. Alexander, 'Early Owners of Torbryan Manor', *Report and Transactions of the Devonshire Association*, **68** (1936), 197-214.

R. Avent, 'The Siege of Laugharne Castle from 28 October to 3 November 1644', in J. R. Kenyon and R. Avent, editors, *Castles in Wales and the Marches* (Cardiff 1987), 185-204.

R. Avent, 'The Early Development of Three Coastal Castles', in H. James, editor, *Sir Gar: Studies in Carmarthenshire History* (Carmarthen 1991), 167-188.

R. Avent, 'The Medieval Development of Laugharne Castle, Dyfed, Wales', *Château Gaillard*, **15** (Caen 1992), 7-18.

J. M. W. Bean, *The Estates of the Percy Family 1416-1537* (Oxford 1958).

R. R. Davies, *Conquest, Coexistence and Change: Wales 1063-1415* (Oxford 1987); reprinted in paperback as, *The Age of Conquest: Wales 1063-1415* (Oxford 1991).

T. Jones, editor, *Brut y Tywysogyon or The Chronicle of the Princes, Peniarth Ms. 20 Version* (Cardiff 1952); *Red Book of Hergest Version* (Cardiff 1955).

J. E. Lloyd, editor, *A History of Carmarthenshire*, volume I, (Cardiff 1935).

R. G. F. Stanes, 'Sir Guy de Brian, K.G.', *Report and Transactions of the Devonshire Association*, **92** (1960), 248-78.

S. Thomas, 'The Descent of the Lordships of Laugharne and Eglwyscummin: Norman Marcher Lordships in South-West Carmarthenshire', *The Carmarthenshire Antiquary*, **6** (1970), 27-52.

R. Turvey, 'Sir John Perrot (1528-1592): A Fourth Centenary Retrospective', *The Journal of the Pembrokeshire Historical Society*, **5** (1992-1993), 14-30.

A book is presented to a prince: a fifteenth-century manuscript illustration (By kind permission of the British Library, Arundel Ms 38, f. 37).